EL PESO HERO
CREATED
HECTOR
RODRIGUEZ III

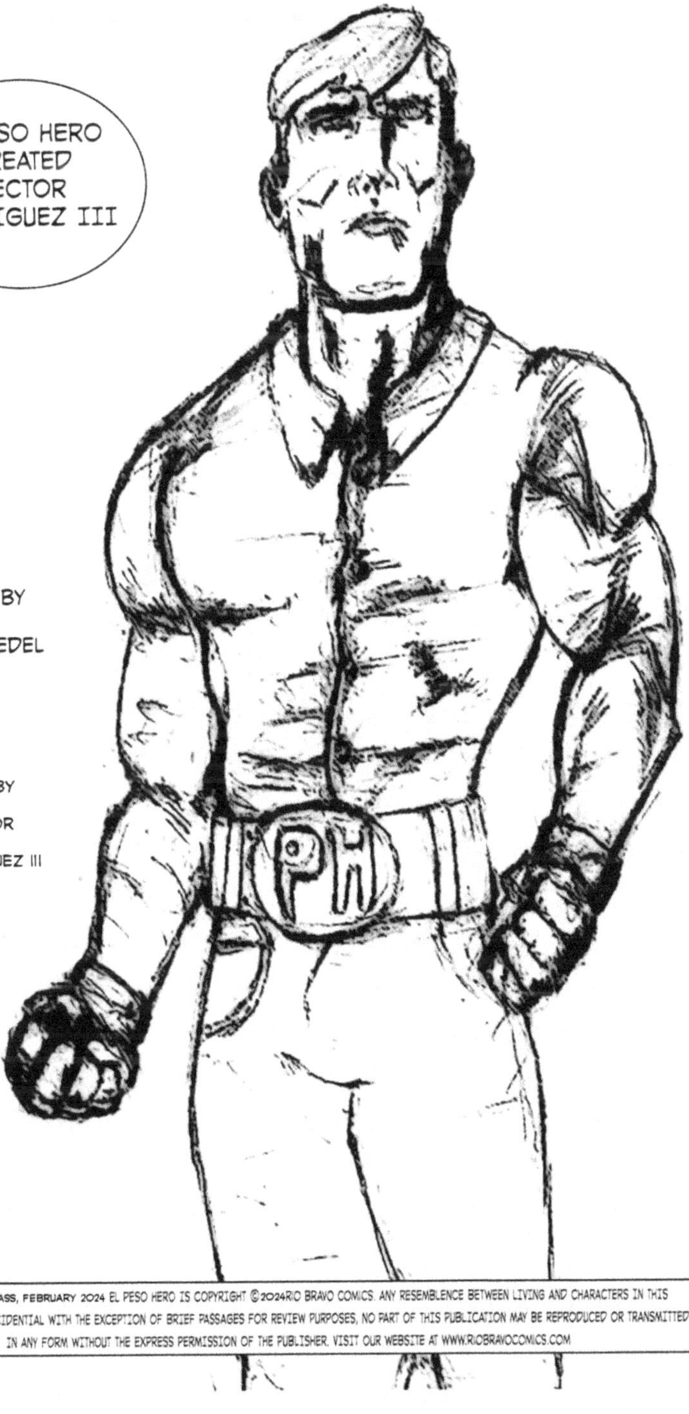

COVER BY

ARIEL MEDEL

ART BY

HECTOR

RODRIGUEZ III

EAGLE PASS, TEXAS.
THE EAGLE PASS AND PIEDRAS NEGRAS, BORDER HAS DEVELOPED INTO THE EPICENTER OF THE 2024 REFUGEE CRISIS FACING THE UNITED STATES.

OKAY, MIJO. YOU STAY RIGHT HERE.

I'LL FIND AWAY AROUND THEM AND COME GET YOU.

GAH!

OH!
NO!
NO!

ARE YOU READY TO CROSS, MIJA?

SIX YEARS AGO MY FAMILY CROSSED.
THEIR JOURNEY FROM HONDURAS WAS PERILOUS.

SAN PEDRO, HONDURAS
SUMMER 2016

VRROOM
TSSSSSSS

ZZZZ
WE NEED TO GO!
BANG!
BANG!
MOM... WHY?
WAKE UP!

WHERE ARE WE GOING? WHERE IS DAD? I WANT DAD!
KPOW
KPOW

BLAM!
BLAM!
THEY TOOK YOUR DAD!

WHO MOM?! WHO!?

WHERE DO YOU THINK YOU ARE GOING? YOUR HUSBAND STILL HAS DEBTS...

2 MILES AWAY FROM GUATEMALA CITY

SQQEEEEKK
WHAT'S GOING ON?!

I AM SO SORRY.

PLEASE HAVE MERCY.

LADIES AND GENTLEMAN, IT IS TIME TO PAY THE TOLL.

TAKE OUT ANY JEWELRY, MONEY, AND ANYTHING OF VALUE.
THE TOP 5 MOST VALUABLE PEOPLE WILL LIVE! HA!

JUST STARE AT THE BUS. DON'T TURN AROUND. I WILL BE RIGHT BACK.

EXCUSE ME YOUNG MAN, I NEED TO GO TO THE RESTROOM.
SIT DOWN OLD LADY.

ARE YOU SERIOUS?!
JUST SHOOT HER!

BREATHE IN, OUT *PHEW*

GUATEMALA CITY
MEXICO CITY
MONTERREY, MEXICO
THESE ARE THE BEST TOURIST VISAS, THEY WILL GET YOU THROUGH THEIR CHECKPOINTS.

NOW, IS OUR TURN TO CROSS.

WHOOOOSH

MAMÁ!
NATALIA!
WHOOOOSH

HELP US!
SHE NEEDS OUR HELP.
DO NOT ENGAGE.

TE TENGO.

VAMOS JUNTOS.

WE HAVE
A HERO IN
OUR MYST.

¿POR
QUÉ NO LAS
SALVARON?

NATALIA!
MAMÁ!

DO NOT COME ANY FURTHER.
POP POP

ELLAS VIENEN BUSCANDO ASILO.

¿LOS AYUDARÁS?

WE WILL ARREST YOU.

BAM

YOU ARE COMING WITH US!

SNAP
ELLOS VIENEN EN PAZ.
WE ARE AUTHORIZE TO USE FORCE!
PUSH THEM BACK!

EL PESO HERO
UCRANIA

No. 1
SEPTEMBER 2016
EL PESO HERO
10¢

EL PESO HERO
SICARIO WAR

AMAZING BORDER STORIES
MC
APPROVED BY THE COMICS CODE AUTHORITY
12¢
15 AUG.
LA PORQUERIA Y ESCORIA AL FINAL SALIO DE SU AGUJERO. LA JUSTICIA TE ESPERA ...
INTRODUCING EL PESO HERO
...YO SOY EL PALADIN DE LA JUSTICIA. YO SOY... EL PESO HERO!
ALSO IN THIS ISSUE
AN IMPORTANT MESSAGE TO YOU, FROM THE RIO BRAVO COMICS TEAM— ABOUT EL PESO HERO!

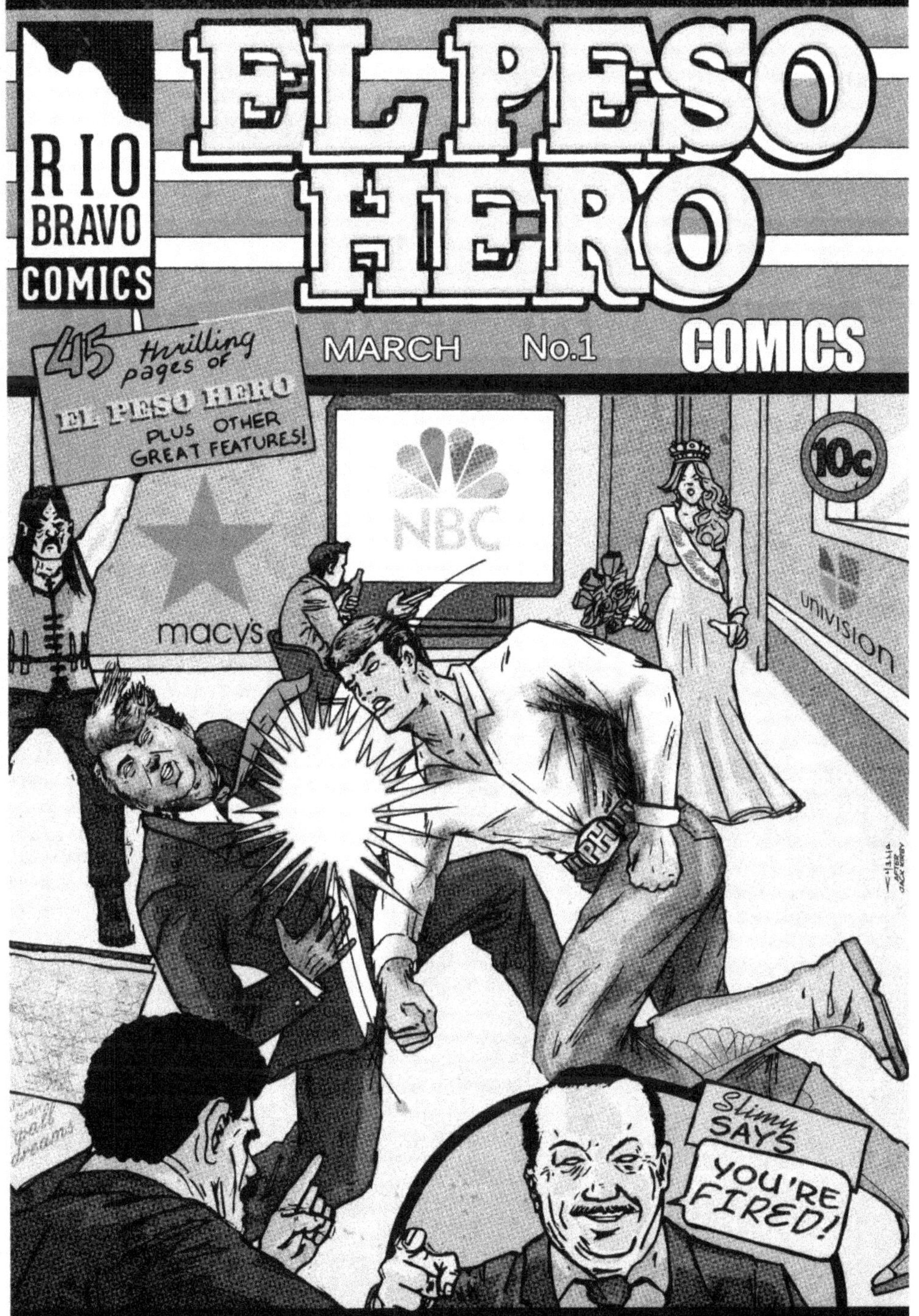

LA COMUNIDAD LATINA SE UNE
RIO BRAVO COMICS
EL PESO HERO
COMICS
MARCH   No.1
45 thrilling pages of EL PESO HERO PLUS OTHER GREAT FEATURES!
NBC
macy's
univision
10c
Slimy SAYS YOU'RE FIRED!
EN CONTRA DEL RACISMO

No. 27
64 PAGES OF ACTION!
SEP 16 2023
El Peso Hero
COMICS
STARTING THIS ISSUE:
THE AMAZING AND UNIQUE ADVENTURES OF
EL PESO HERO!

EL PESO HERO
RISE OF MEXICO CITY
COMING SOON